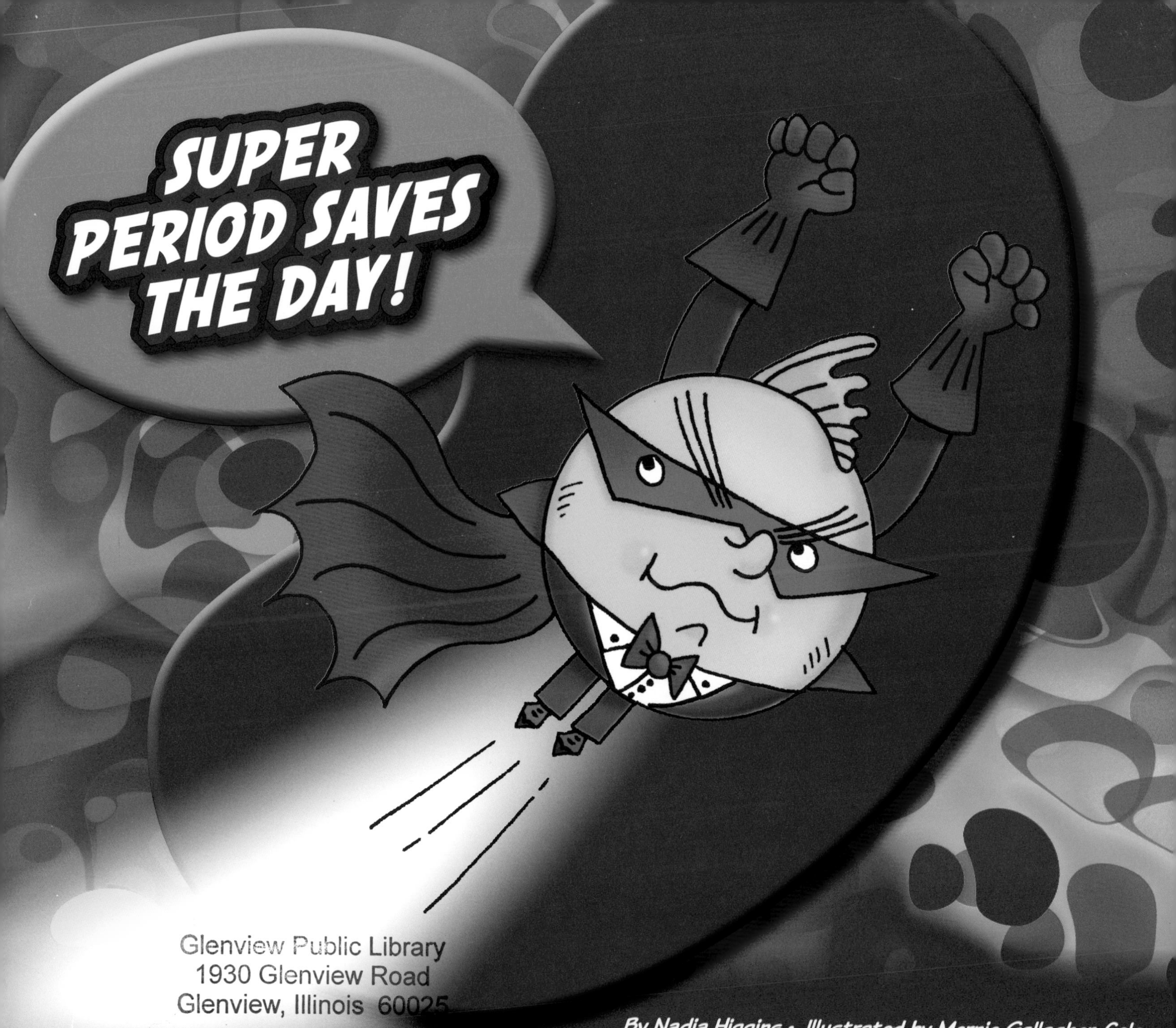

By Nadia Higgins • Illustrated by Mernie Gallagher-Cole

The Child's World®

Published by The Child's World®
1980 Lookout Drive • Mankato, MN 56003-1705
800-599-READ • www.childsworld.com

Acknowledgments
The Child's World®: Mary Berendes, Publishing Director
The Design Lab: Design and production
Red Line Editorial: Editorial direction

Design elements: Billyfoto/Dreamstime;
Dan Ionut Popescu/Dreamstime

ISBN 9781614732709
LCCN 2012932875

Printed in the United States of America
Mankato, MN
July 2012
PA02117

About the Author: Nadia Higgins is a children's book author based in Minneapolis, Minnesota. Nadia has been a punctuation fan since the age of five, when she first wrote "Happy Birthday!" on a homemade card. "I love punctuation because it is both orderly and expressive," Nadia says. Her dream is to visit Punctuation Junction someday.

About the Illustrator: Mernie Gallagher-Cole is a freelance children's book illustrator living outside of Philadelphia. She has illustrated many children's books. Mernie enjoys punctuation marks so much that she uses a hyphen in her last name!

It was a clear, crisp morning in Punctuation Junction. Super Period sat down in his big, soft chair with a plop. Then he opened his laptop to read the news. "*Ahhhhhh,*" he sighed.

The pleased period began to read, until— "AAAAAARRRGHHH!" The superhero jumped to his feet. "C . . . L!" he gasped. "Look . . . at . . . this!"

"Oh dear," the capital letter fairy said. "What's happened to the periods and capital letters?"

CL read the news story about the big parade in Punctuation Junction. "Does the parade begin at three or four? What is a prize period? Oh my, I can hardly make sense of this at all," CL said.

"Somebody is trying to spoil tomorrow's period parade," Super Period said. "I have to stop them."

The superhero shot into town with CL close behind. First stop was the news office.

"Punctuation!" Super Period called out to the reporters. "What happened?"

"I'm not sure," Karen said with alarm. "Without periods, everything's a jumble."

"The periods were here one moment," added Arnie slowly. "Then they were all rolling into a bag. Or were they scooped up with a spoon?"

"There was something green, I think," said Petunia. "A green tree with a pink hat?"

"Or an evil green pencil," Super Period said. "Sounds like the work of Evil Pete."

"Which way did he go?" CL asked the reporters. "Was it north, or maybe south, or southeast?"

Super Period squeezed his eyes shut. "Period power—activate!" His round body jiggled from thinking so hard. "Where would Evil Pete take the periods?" he asked himself. When he opened his eyes, the answer was clear. "Of course!" he said, pointing at Arnie's sweater.

"To the polka dot factory!" Super Period cried.

He and CL shot across town. They went to the giant dotted building.

They sneaked inside the factory. "How will we ever find the periods here?" CL worried.

"You'll never find them!" A green pencil jumped out from behind a dress.

"Evil Pete!" CL cried.

"I've created the perfect period prison," the bad pencil said in a soft, scratchy voice. "They're mine forever, Super Period! The period parade is ruined. *Ah-ha-ha-ha-ha*!" With that, he scribbled on the floor.

"Never fear!" cried Super Period. And with the force of *good sense,* a dash of *clear ideas,* and some *read aloud power,* Super Period freed the periods.

"Attack!" the
periods shouted.
"I'll be back!"
Evil Pete screamed
as he ran away. But
he could hardly be
heard above the roar
of the angry periods.

With the periods back in place, the news story was fixed.

The whole city is abuzz with excitement. Tomorrow the period parade begins at three. Four capital letters will be on hand to kick off the fun. Events include a neatest handwriting contest. Bring a fact for the fact jar and you may win a prize. Period lovers, get ready to enjoy the town's most orderly and educational event of the year.

And everyone found their way to the parade right at three.

What Is a Sentence?

A sentence is a group of words that makes sense all by itself. All sentences start with capital letters. If the sentence tells a fact or makes a comment, it ends in a period.

SENTENCE
(makes sense by itself)

Evil Pete is the meanest pencil in the land.
I hope I win the neatest handwriting contest.
Periods rock.

NOT A SENTENCE
(doesn't make sense by itself)

Evil Pete is
I hope I
rock

Evil Pete loves to annoy periods. He writes words that do not make sentences. Can you add words to turn his gibberish into sentences? Do not forget to start each one with a capital letter. Finish each with a neat, round period.

polka-dotted toenails
riding on the back of a Dalmatian
don't you ever
when you least expect me
and then you won't
this is harder than
round, lovely, bouncy, and smart
interestingly evil
deliciously evil
a period is not
the best way to
to tickle a pencil

DO NOT WRITE IN THE BOOK!

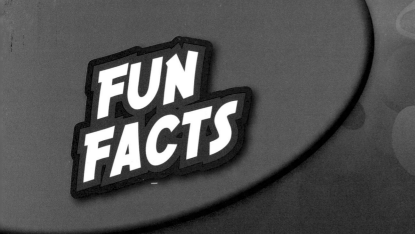

FUN FACTS

Another Name

People in England use periods the same way we do. But they have a different name for the tiny, round mark. They call it a *full stop*.

Mr. Punctuation

A period's main job is to end a sentence. But it also helps out with some short words, such as *Mr.* and *Mrs.* These words stand for longer ones. *Mr.* is short for *Mister*. *Mrs.* is short for *Mistress*.

Math Help

A period is also used in math. It is called a decimal point. The numbers to the right of the decimal point are less than one. Decimals are used in money math. For example, $10.95 means you have 10 dollars and 95 cents.

Back in Time

The history of punctuation goes back to ancient Greece. Written marks showed speakers how long to pause when saying a speech. The mark that got the longest pause was the period.